Meet My Pet

HEDGEHOG

AV2
www.openlightbox.com

Jared Siemens

1-Year K–5 Subscription
ISBN 978-1-7911-3320-7

Meet My Pet

HEDGEHOG

CONTENTS

Meet My Pet

HEDGEHOG

CONTENTS

I want a pet hedgehog.

I need to learn how
to take care of him.

There are many different kinds of hedgehogs.

Most hedgehogs are colored brown, black, and white.

BODY PARTS

My hedgehog is covered in sharp spines.

He curls into a little ball if he is scared.

ARE THEY SCARED?

Hedgehogs roll into a **BALL**.

Turtles hide in their **SHELLS**.

Hamsters **RUN** away.

Guinea pigs stay **STILL**.

My pet hedgehog will live in a cage.

I will help clean his cage once a week.

My pet hedgehog will use a wheel in his cage to exercise.

I will let him out of his cage to play every day.

My pet hedgehog will need to eat special hedgehog food.

I will feed him once a day.

My pet hedgehog will need baths to stay clean.

I will give him a bath when he is dirty.

My pet hedgehog will sleep all day.

I will keep him in a quiet space so he can get plenty of rest.

Growing Up

Newborn Hedgehog
A few hours of age
His spines are hidden under his skin.
He drinks milk from his mother.

Hoglet
About 5 weeks of age
He eats solid food.
He loses his baby spines.

Young Hedgehog
About 12 weeks of age
He is playful.
He digs and runs.

Adult Hedgehog
About 2 years of age
He is active at night.
He eats treats.

I am ready to take home my pet hedgehog.

I will take good care of him.

THINK ABOUT IT!

What other steps can you take to keep your hedgehog happy and healthy?

HEDGEHOG FACTS

These pages provide detailed information that expands on the interesting facts found in the book. They are intended to be used by adults as a learning support to help young readers round out their knowledge of each amazing animal featured in the *Meet My Pet* series.

Pages 4–5

I want a pet hedgehog. Hedgehogs are named for their unique foraging behavior, which involves rooting through hedges and undergrowth in search of insects and worms. They make pig-like grunts while they search for food. Hedgehogs are found in nature across Africa, Europe, and Asia. They are seen as an exotic pet and are still illegal to own in some cities and states. Where it is legal to keep hedgehogs as pets, their popularity has risen by more than 50 percent in recent years.

Pages 6–7

There are many different kinds of hedgehogs. There are about 15 species of hedgehog. Nearly all of the pet hedgehogs in the United States are African pygmy hedgehogs. Adult hedgehogs weigh between 6 ounces and 32 ounces (170 and 907 grams) and grow between 6 and 9 inches (15 and 23 centimeters) long. A hedgehog's quills and hair can be several different colors, including brown, black, cream, and gray. Albino hedgehogs have red eyes, as well as completely white quills and hair.

Pages 8–9

My hedgehog is covered in sharp spines. A hedgehog is covered in stiff spines, or quills, except on its face, legs, and underside. The average hedgehog has between 5,000 and 7,000 spines, which account for 35 percent of its total body weight. There are two muscles in a hedgehog's back that raise and lower its spines. When a hedgehog is scared, it can curl up into a ball with the quills facing outward to protect itself. Many hedgehogs also curl into a ball to sleep.

Pages 10–11

My pet hedgehog will live in a cage. Hedgehogs can be very active. They need a large enough cage to give them space to move around. The minimum recommended size for a hedgehog cage is 4 square feet (0.4 square meters). Wire cages with a bottom set into a deep pan offer proper ventilation and are easy to clean. Fabric for burrowing, such as fleece or other soft materials, will keep your hedgehog comfortable. Hedgehogs may also enjoy a small enclosure that mimics a burrow.

Pages 12–13

My pet hedgehog will use a wheel in his cage to exercise. In nature, hedgehogs can travel up to 7 miles (11 kilometers) in a single night. It is important that your hedgehog has something it can use for exercise, such as a wheel. The best wheel for a pet hedgehog will have a solid bottom. The majority of a pet hedgehog's activity will take place at night. It is best to keep a hedgehog where it can be active without waking up anyone in the house.

Pages 14–15

My pet hedgehog will need to eat special hedgehog food. Hedgehogs need a diet high in protein and low in fat. They need two bowls of food, one dry and one wet, in their cage at all times. Cat food that is made primarily of beef or chicken is the best food option for your hedgehog. A water bottle is also necessary to keep a hedgehog well hydrated. Hedgehogs enjoy an occasional treat. Farm-raised mealworms or crickets can be good treat options for your pet.

Pages 16–17

My pet hedgehog will need baths to stay clean. Hedgehogs do not groom themselves like other animals do. Instead, they cover themselves in their own saliva, a habit called "anointing." Some experts believe a hedgehog does this because it likes the smell of something it ate, or it is trying to mask its natural scent. Most hedgehogs only require one bath a month. Even though hedgehogs are natural swimmers, it is important not to leave your hedgehog alone in the bathtub or sink.

Pages 18–19

My pet hedgehog will sleep all day. Hedgehogs are nocturnal, meaning they are awake at night and asleep during the day. While some hedgehogs adapt to daytime activity, many will spend their entire day asleep. Baby hedgehogs, called hoglets, sleep quite a bit, especially after moving to a new home. Some hedgehogs display crepuscular behavior, meaning they are most active at dawn and dusk.

Pages 20–21

I am ready to take home my pet hedgehog. Hedgehogs are solitary animals that are easily frightened. It will take time for a hedgehog to adjust to a new home. Once your hedgehog is comfortable, it is okay to begin handling it. You can do so by scooping it up with both hands. Unlike some pets, hedgehogs do not need regular vaccinations. However, it is important to take your hedgehog for a checkup at the veterinarian before bringing it home.

KEY WORDS

Research has shown that as much as 65 percent of all written material published in English is made up of 300 words. These 300 words cannot be taught using pictures or learned by sounding them out. They must be recognized by sight. This book contains 70 common sight words to help young readers improve their reading fluency and comprehension. This book also teaches young readers several important content words, such as proper nouns. These words are paired with pictures to aid in learning and improve understanding.

Page	Sight Words First Appearance
5	a, him, how, I, learn, need, of, take, to, want
6	and, are, different, kinds, many, most, there, white
7	parts
8	he, if, in, into, is, little, my
9	away, run, still, their, they
10	help, his, live, once, will
12	day, every, let, out, play, use
14	eat, food
16	give, when
18	all, can, get, keep, so
19	at, about, few, from, mother, night, under, up, years, young
21	am, good, home, it, other, think, what, you, your

Page	Content Words First Appearance
5	hedgehog
7	belly, ear, leg, nose, snout, spines
8	ball
9	guinea pigs, hamsters, shells, turtles
10	cage, week
12	wheel
16	baths
18	rest, space
19	hoglet, hours, milk, skin, treats
21	steps

Published by Lightbox Learning Inc.
276 5th Avenue, Suite 704 #917
New York, NY 10001
Website: www.openlightbox.com

Library of Congress Control Number: 2023933094

ISBN 978-1-7911-5603-9 (hardcover)
ISBN 978-1-7911-5604-6 (softcover)
ISBN 978-1-7911-5605-3 (multi-user eBook)

Printed in Guangzhou, China
1 2 3 4 5 6 7 8 9 0 27 26 25 24 23

062023
100922

Project Coordinator: Sara Cucini Art Director: Terry Paulhus

Every reasonable effort has been made to trace ownership and to obtain permission to reprint copyright material. The publisher would be pleased to have any errors or omissions brought to its attention so that they may be corrected in subsequent printings.

The publisher acknowledges Getty Images, Alamy, and Shutterstock as the primary image suppliers for this title.